# THE CHOICE

by

**Jock Macneish and Tony Richardson**

D1641931

First published by DONT PRESS Australia 1993
Second Impression 1994  Third Impression 1995
European Edition 1994   Chinese Edition 1995
Fourth Impression 2000

ISBN 0 646 15878 9

Published and distributed by DONT PRESS
14 Hawkes Road, Warrandyte, Victoria 3113.
Victoria Ph : 03 9844 4164  Fax : 03 9844 4520
Tasmania Ph : 03 6297 1199  Fax : 03 6297 1322
e-mail : dont.press@tassie.net.au
and : macneish@hilink.com.au
http:/www.dontpress.com

This book is copyright and no part should be reproduced without permission.
However, the authors are happy to offer automatic permission to anyone who wishes to reproduce
the material from the book, provided that the ideas remain whole and that the work is correctly attributed.
Inquiries should be addressed to the publisher.

Produced and printed in Australia using recycled papers.

# FOREWORD

I met Tony Richardson in Melbourne at Workplace Australia in 1991. We got some beer and hamburgers, took a table by the stream where we could watch the ducks, and traded war stories - the "change wars," not the heavy weapons kind. ( The best change war weapons, of course, are not heavy at all, but light and light-hearted, like this book. ) Tony told me of his adventures in making things better, starting with the family paper mill. It sounded a lot like my family printing business where I spent the 1960's putting together self-managing work teams when, according to my folk-singing friends, I should have been doing sex, drugs and rock and roll. Instead, I developed a keen appreciation of hands-on industry and working people that qualified me - 25 years later - to have a beer with Richardson. And so we found parallels in our beliefs that business can make money *and* provide people with good work. Indeed, humane workplaces often boast the greatest economic success and the best track record with new technologies.

When I got back to the states I found my mail stuffed with cartoons from Oz. It was funny stuff drawn by Jock Macneish that had both a point and an edge. The cartoons got at our organisational and bureaucratic foibles, inclinations and practices. They put irrational organisational stuff we all take for granted in a funny, albeit disconcerting new light. I found myself faced with the diligent fruit polisher asking "Do I do that too?" Or of the business chimneys, "Why do I put up with that nonsense?"

Eric Trist, my friend and mentor on whose shoulders I have climbed for many years, believed deep in his Celtic soul that organisational structures/processes/functions result from "choice, not chance". Eric thought we could choose whole, integrated, cooperative work systems over the alternatives so graphically delineated by Jock and Tony under a new job classification called "fruit polishing."

Fred Emery, Trist's erstwhile collaborator, has preached for years on the split between two opposing, and contradictory design principles. The first--one person, one task--leads to the unhappy characters spread across these pages. The second--one person, multiple skills and broad knowledge--leads to a very different sort of work system. Inevitably making the second choice leads us away from external, coercive supervision toward the responsible internal supervisor lurking in each one of us. It is the latter that Jock and Tony advocate. Pride, dignity and meaning in work are abstractions that come alive only when we have control of our own work and workplaces, enough control, say, to be free to do the right thing without having to ask a senior fruit polisher for permission.

Now I happen to believe that every person does the best they can with what they have. If you work for, manage, or supervise a fruit polishing operation, like it or not, you're doing the best you can with what you've got. I trust you will have well-polished fruit. None of us changes anything about our lives - jobs, spouses, education, friends - until we are ready, willing and able. Sometimes life has to get worse before we make it better. And not all workplaces are such pure cases of mindlessness run amok as in the dreary brickworks and slave galleys depicted here.

Jock and Tony say this book is for innovators. I say there's an innovator in all of us. Does that mean this book is for everyone? Hell, no. In all of us there's also a stick-in-the-mud, dig-in-your-heels, I-don't-have-time-for-all-that-idealistic garbage fruit-polisher.

Which part of you is running your show today? If it's your innovator self, ready, willing and able to choose a different kind of workplace, you'd do well to spend an hour with your new friends Macneish and Richardson.

Marvin Weisbord

# Contents

INTRODUCTION..................................................................................4

THE CHOICE 1 - ASSUMPTIONS OR VALUES................................................8

THE CHOICE 2 - PROBLEMS OR SYSTEMS :
               EXPERTS OR *EVERYBODY*..................................................18

THE CHOICE 3 - FRAGMENTATION OR WHOLENESS...................................30

THE CHOICE 4 - BARRIERS OR BOUNDARIES...........................................40

THE CHOICE 5 - SAFE PAST OR RISKY FUTURE........................................48

THE CHOICE 6 - RULES OR RESULTS......................................................68

THE CHOICE 7 - ENVIRONMENT : DEMOTIVATING OR MOTIVATING...74

THE CHOICE 8 - LOOKS NEW OR REALLY NEW.......................................92

BIOGRAPHIES AND ACKNOWLEDGEMENTS...................................................98

# Introduction

This guide is for innovators. It is for people who know that traditional workplaces are at best crazy and at worst inhumane and barbaric. It is for people who find the way they have to work frustrating.

It is for people who can't give up wanting a better work system.
Try this test. What percentage of your creativity, your cleverness, your capacity to contribute, and your spirituality, do you leave at the door as you walk into work?

If your answer is over 50% read on. If not save yourself the time and money.

This Guide is the first part of a trilogy.
This is the "WHAT" of Workplace Improvement.
The next will be a Guide on the "HOW".
The third will be a Guide to the "WHAT THEN".

# A Guide for the Journey

We hope this guide will do five things.

1. Confirm for you that traditional workplaces can't work.
2. Provide some ways to think differently about work.
3. Provide some confidence that frustration about work, in its traditional form, is not a sign of lunacy, but a sign of life.
4. Point to some of the fundamentals that will make workplaces work.
5. Make less daunting but more imperative the task of involving *Everybody* in improving the whole system.

If this guide prompts some smiles about traditional work organisations that is all to the good. Sometimes we need to laugh at things before we can change them.

# THE CHOICE 1 - ASSUMPTIONS OR VALUES

- MORE THAN ONCE UPON A TIME
- VALUES
- LOST AT THE BEGINNING OF THE JOURNEY
- VISION BEFORE STRUCTURE

# More than once upon a time

A decade ago, one of Australia's large industrial workplaces was in crisis. There was palpable distrust between 'workers' and 'management' and productivity reflected this. The Training Manager indicated his side's view when he called the workers "That mob of cretinous morons". The problem, it was assumed, was low commitment and low skills among the workers.

In its dying months there was an enlightened program of involving employees in trying to save the place. Some people were engaged to collect ideas. The queue for appointments was endless but it proved too late and closure was announced. Some weeks afterwards one of the people who had been collecting the ideas met an elderly tradesman who reached into his pocket and pulled out a few sheets of paper, "I know the decision's made" he said, "but I still want to give to someone what I think we could have done to fix up this place." No commitment?

In earlier days an auditor had been installed to create a list of stolen items. He concluded there was enough missing to build a forty foot boat. It was found later, well made out of pilfered materials. No skills?

The workers had as inaccurate a view of the managers as the managers had of them.

That workplace had spent sixty years making assumptions. The result was a tragedy for its people and its community.

THE CHOICE 1 - ASSUMPTIONS OR VALUES

# Values

There are two systems for work. They are based on different values and they value people in different ways. In the traditional work organisation people are a cost, a necessary extension to its assets.

In the new work system people are the assets and the controllers of their technology.

One system creates flexibility by hiring and firing people. The other creates flexibility by developing highly skilled and flexible people.

The beliefs that support these values are just as different.

THE CHOICE 1 - ASSUMPTIONS OR VALUES

| Old system | New system |
|---|---|
| **Beliefs**....... distrust | **Beliefs**.......... trust |
| authority and status | respect and roles |
| uniformity (one best way) | equifinality (many good ways) |
| simplicity | complexity |

People can work in traditional organisations, even at senior levels, and hate the beliefs and values that drive their workplace. They will be in constant overt or covert conflict. They will experience enormous personal stress. They, like most, are victims of their system.

# Lost at the beginning of the journey

The people in this picture tell a story about change. The old system is behind them. The new system is through a fog. The people are confused.

Although they are 'lost at the beginning of their journey', they are setting out with the best possible beginning. They have explored and agreed how they would like their workplace to be. They are clear about their ideals and what they value.

**When we are clear about where we are going, we can work from imagination, rather than habit.**

Values endure. They are more stable than needs.

THE CHOICE 1 - ASSUMPTIONS OR VALUES

## Vision before structure

*Everybody* has and seeks ideals, We all have a vision for what might be. We create community when we share vision. So structures that isolate and fragment act to impede workplace community. When that happens, it hurts to have a vision.

People's go beyond issues of pay and profit. They encompass things like commitment pride, community, service and care for the environment.

Shared visions create clear determination which will go beyond winning, bigness and best. It will not be about the organisation being enriched by the presence of society, but about society being enriched by the presence of the organisation.

People's visions of 'what might be' can either frustrate them, or if shared, will energise and unite them.

THE CHOICE 1 - ASSUMPTIONS OR VALUES

## THE CHOICE 2 - PROBLEMS OR SYSTEMS : EXPERTS OR *EVERYBODY*

- THE LEARNING CURVE

- SYSTEMS. TOUCH THEM ANYWHERE TOUCH THEM EVERYWHERE

- THE CHOICE. EITHER CHANGE THE SYSTEM OR POLISH THE FRUIT

- THE FRUIT POLISHER'S PARADE

- THE HIGH-TECH GALLEY

# The learning curve

In this century we have learned two vital things about working together.

First, when we solve problems we merely stop losing. Problem solving requires standing in the present and looking backwards. When we do this for long we get lost, overwhelmed and depressed. When we solve one problem we usually find we have created another. We need to solve problems. But the most powerful results will come when we link the problem through to its effect on the whole system.

Second, experts can create solutions and write in people's parts. But they cannot incorporate the insights, wisdom and experience of *Everybody* and they cannot guarantee that people will play their assigned parts.

We need experts. But the most powerful learning and the smoothest implementation will occur when *Everybody* and experts work together.

We need to bring experts and *Everybody* together and link problem solving to whole system improvement. Our present challenge for workplace improvement is to create processes that encircle everything that's affected and include *Everybody* who's affected.

THE CHOICE  2  - PROBLEMS OR SYSTEMS, EXPERTS OR *EVERYBODY*

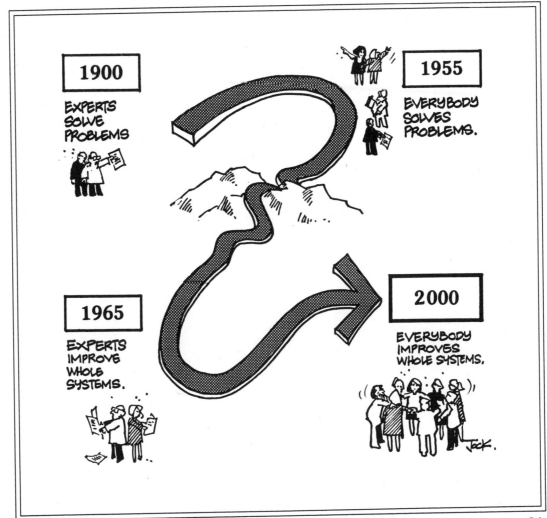

ACKNOWLEDGEMENT TO MARVIN WEISBORD

## Systems. Touch them anywhere - touch them everywhere

All systems are interconnected. A change anywhere will be felt everywhere. You can't easily isolate a little bit and just fix that. To change anything we may have to change everything. Whole system change.

Whole system change can overawe because it affects *Everybody*

Innovators find it difficult to stay back. They, like the person in the picture, may decide to hop in. But the minute they touch anything alarm bells ring everywhere.

That's why innovators find traditional organisations a struggle.

THE CHOICE 2 - PROBLEMS OR SYSTEMS, EXPERTS OR *EVERYBODY*

# The Choice. Either change the system or polish the fruit

Many attempts to improve organisations are simply " fruit polishing"

The source of the problem is not in the fruit. It is how it came to be that way. The person on the ladder is too close to the symptoms to be able to focus on the cause.

The cause of the problem is the system, the toxic waste dump.

Programs that fail to change the system will change little. Change which addresses the system may seem ambitious, but anything less, however plausible, is illusory.

It is 'fruit polishing'.

THE CHOICE  2  - PROBLEMS OR SYSTEMS, EXPERTS OR *EVERYBODY*

## Fruit polisher's parade

Fruit polishing does not change the system. It is not felt at the roots of the problem.

Products for fruit polishing usually come in very glossy binders. They often arrive 'jet-fresh' from a long way away. They are well known for their abbreviations. Some places can create an alphabet soup with them. They follow each other like floats in a parade. They promise as much as they cost; a hell of a lot.

Fruit polishing may cause a commotion but the system remains untouched. In a few months the roots will recreate the essence of what was there before, plus cynicism.

The old system is frighteningly strong. It can tame most of our best endeavours to change it. It has tamed the Technological Revolution. In the main, computers haven't been used to change the way we work, just to automate it. They too have been used to polish fruit.

High-Tech fruit polish !

THE CHOICE  2  - PROBLEMS OR SYSTEMS, EXPERTS OR *EVERYBODY*

# THE CHOICE 3 - FRAGMENTATION OR WHOLENESS

- THE RELATIONSHIPS WHICH MAKE WORKPLACES WORK

- THE ORGANISATIONAL PAWN

- FRAGMENTATION OR WHOLENESS

- STRUCTURAL REVIEWS

## The relationships which make workplaces work

There are three parts to organisations: People, Technologies and Business results. The quality of an organisation's success is a reflection of the quality of the relationship between these three parts.

It is difficult to establish and maintain these whole system relationships. This is because humans are possessive about territory. We create corners and view the world from them. Since most people work in only one of the parts they view the system from their part. They rarely check what the view is like from the other parts.

Traditional organisations set up the following pattern:

The Business Results People work with figures, trends, priorities and customer information. On the basis of these they make decisions about new investments and hand on to:

The Technical Department who, as we heard it put once, "design it, build it, bolt it down and piss off".

By now the fitting of people to the technology has become a problem. This is handed over to the Human Resource Department.

THE CHOICE 3 - FRAGMENTATION OR WHOLENESS

ACKNOWLEDGEMENT TO MARVIN WEISBORD

## The organisational pawn

Adults don't thrill to being pawns in someone else's chess game. To stop creating pawns we need to move from thinking 'tasks' to thinking 'relationships'.

To make this change, the hub of the new system becomes the information system, 'the good oil'. This provides whole system understanding to all of the parts. It gives the data for the relationships.

'The good oil' is a new type of information system. It uses computers to support a new type of work organisation, not to automate the old one.

It is not merely a management information system (MIS). A MIS is designed only for the managers, often the business results people. The new system requires an organisation information system.

*Everybody* contributes what they know at their point in the system. *Everybody* has access to all of the information.

THE CHOICE 3 - FRAGMENTATION OR WHOLENESS

## Fragmentation or Wholeness

The old system creates fragmented workplaces.

Despite people's best endeavours, multitudes of tedious meetings and forests of internal memoranda, systems, once fragmented, will always defy integration.

In fragmented workplaces people know where they fit in but not how their contribution fits in. People can rarely see the big picture. *Everybody* grumbles about communications.

In fragmented workplaces, people cannot create ' the relationships which make workplaces work.'

## Structural reviews

Dozens of people have seen this picture and said "Oh no, that's exactly what we've done !".

Organisations need to change structures. But too often structural change is designed by 'experts' and imposed by managers.

In these cases, people whose daily working lives are deeply affected are victims in the process. They are pawns. They can only influence by resisting.

There is an infinite variety of structures that an organisation can try. Changing structures is cosmetic unless it removes barriers and creates whole system thinking and whole system co-operation.

Structural change, unless it is part of whole system change, is a very expensive way to change very little.

THE CHOICE 3 - FRAGMENTATION OR WHOLENESS

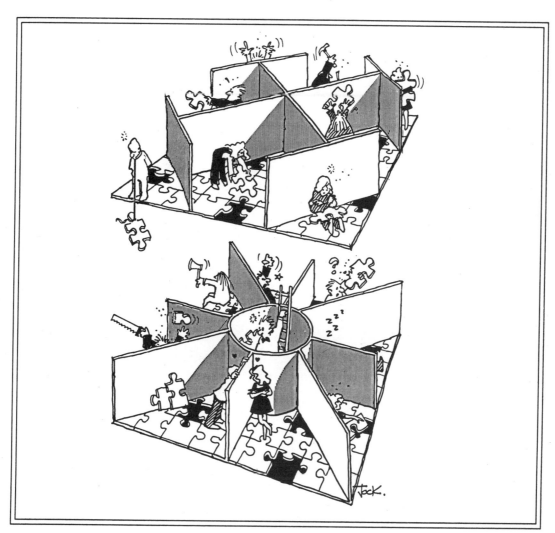

# THE CHOICE 4 - BARRIERS OR BOUNDARIES

- VERTICAL BARRIERS
- HORIZONTAL BARRIERS
- BOUNDARIES

# Vertical barriers

Traditional thinking creates bureaucracy and hierarchy and these inevitably create barriers.

Bureaucracy is designed on the principle that no one may do anything unless a person at least one position higher says they may. The word hierarchy comes from the two Greek words, *hieros* meaning sacred and *arkhes* ruler. Sacred rulers? Hierarchy is elitist, it is a measure of status and therefore can be a measure of relative contempt.

Barriers are imposed, impermeable and based on a past rationality. They manifest distrust. They always frustrate co-operation, enquiry and learning.

Barriers intimidate, that is the essence of their power. They are reinforced by the ignorance they create. They can also create a special breed of 'clever' employees who, because they thrive in the mess of fragmentation, create that sort of mess to thrive. These people are often known as 'good operators'!

Vertical barriers create places for people to bully, hide and snooze. Manifestations are rank, dining quarters, paper qualifications, tenure, cars and spots to park them.

THE CHOICE 4 - BARRIERS OR BOUNDARIES

# Horizontal barriers

Organisations which have a passion about their structure usually end up with a labyrinth of horizontal barriers. The traditional names of sub-structures indicate and support barriers: Department, Division, Branch, Section, Unit and the like.

These sort of structures and their titles advocate specialness and provincial thinking.

Intra-company rivalries, the 'classic' phone around, divisional responsibility, divisions of labour and union demarcations are examples of horizontal barriers within a fragmented organisation.

The move from barriers to boundaries is a move from fragmentation to wholeness. From single tasks to many tasks and from people working at a function, to teams working with many tasks and a whole system.

THE CHOICE 4 - BARRIERS OR BOUNDARIES

## Boundaries

Boundaries are negotiated, changeable and set up to make the system work well, today. They require and create trust.

Boundaries are necessary because *Everybody* cannot do everything and be everywhere. But these boundaries must be permeable. Boundaries must be established in a way that allows *Everybody* to know enough about the whole system to know how what they do affects it. *Everybody* must also have enough autonomy to be able to make decisions in the interest of the whole.

Boundaries require that people manage themselves as adults and act towards each other with respect. This includes people co-operating across their boundaries and respecting the protocol involved in crossing them.

An essential part of the shift to a new work organisation is the shift from barriers to boundaries.
The old barriers were set around 'one person one task', discrete functions and individualised responsibilities. The new boundaries are set around 'a workteam, many tasks' and 'whole system' functions and responsibilities.

THE CHOICE 4 - BARRIERS OR BOUNDARIES

## THE CHOICE 5 - SAFE PAST OR RISKY FUTURE

- THE FOUR ROOM APARTMENT
- FOUR LEVELS OF GROUP MATURITY

# The four room apartment

*Everybody* in every aspect of their life, is travelling through the phases represented in this 'four room apartment'.
Workplaces go through these phases too. These are the sorts of the phrases that are heard in each room

Contentment Room: "Work's going well". "I hope I can serve out my days here". "It's nice to be able to see where we're going".

Denial Room: "There's a downturn but it'll go away". "This is not our problem". "Why do we need to change?".

Confusion Room: "What the hell do we do now ?" "Nobody seems to have any answers to things any more". "I can't imagine how we got into this mess".

Renewal Room: "Let's ..." "Why not...?." "I've got a fantastic idea..."

There is only one 'unhealthy' room, the Denial Room. The rest are part of the seasonal landscape of any living organisation. Some people, in a sort of kindly way, might aspire to hold their organisation in the Contentment Room. Beware of too much of this sort of kindliness!

THE CHOICE 5 - SAFE PAST OR RISKY FUTURE

ACKNOWLEDGEMENT TO CLAES JANSSEN AND MARVIN WEISBORD

# The Contentment Room

The Contentment Room may at first seem the most desirable room. It's not, it's just a good room to rest in. *Everybody* needs to take stock or even snooze once in a while.

It is pleasant for people to have time in this room but they may need to beware.

The next room is the Denial Room.

By definition we enter it without realising.

THE CHOICE 5 - SAFE PAST OR RISKY FUTURE

ACKNOWLEDGEMENT TO CLAES JANSSEN AND MARVIN WEISBORD

# The Denial Room

The Denial Room is sometimes necessary within our private lives. It can provide some rest when reality is too harsh and brutal to face just now. But the Denial Room can host disaster for organisations. It is the room in which Organisations go broke.

There is nothing good about this room. It is boring, enervating and soulless.
The occupants are dining out on yesterdays good ideas. Staying there requires something between blindness and dishonesty but leaving requires courage. There is only one exit, to the Confusion Room, so people bank up against that door. It is bloody hard for some of us to admit we 'don't know what to do'. And yet that is the entry condition for the next room.

People in the Denial Room may respond to questions and information but they won't respond to advice. They won't hear it. They need data and to be able to look out and around so they can gain their own conviction that they must move.

The Contentment and Denial Rooms have little energy in them. The next two have plenty.

THE CHOICE 5 - SAFE PAST OR RISKY FUTURE

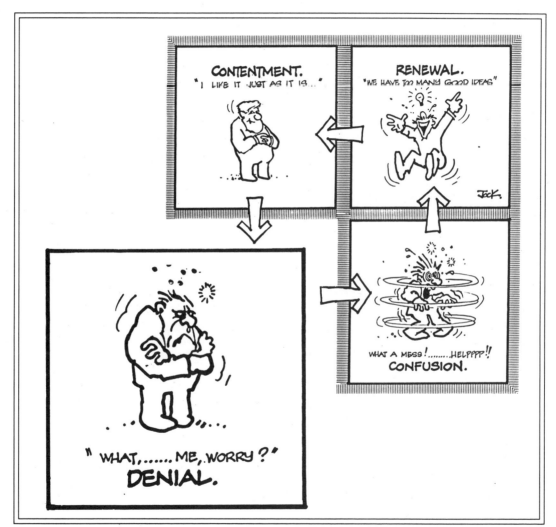

ACKNOWLEDGEMENT TO CLAES JANSSEN AND MARVIN WEISBORD

# The Confusion Room

Being in the Confusion Room is stressful, uncomfortable and even emotional. In fact, it can be sheer hell. But somehow this room is the central dynamo of improvement. The degree of confusion determines the degree of improvement. Renewal originates from here. There is a danger some people may try to escape from the intensity of this room. But they can only escape back to denial. They do this by blaming or jumping to solutions.
An organisation will probably do best here if they 'get the whole system in the room'. It will take courage to be honest, stay together and not run away. It may help to structure tasks and it will certainly help to focus on the future.

The Confusion Room invites problem solving questions like "What's wrong?", "How have we failed?", "Who mucked up?", etc. But these questions require that we look back not forward. They focus on bits, not the whole; on discrete problems, not on the system. They are recipes for blurred focus, blaming, inactivity and powerlessness. They lead back to the Denial Room.

There are other questions that point forward and lead to a search for solutions. These questions can have greatest positive effect if they include a search for an ideal. Questions like "What would it be like if we got it right?" "What has worked so far that we could build on ?" and even "What's missing?"

THE CHOICE 5 - SAFE PAST OR RISKY FUTURE

ACKNOWLEDGEMENT TO CLAES JANSSEN AND MARVIN WEISBORD

# The Renewal Room

The Renewal Room is fantastic. Like the confusion room it has very high energy but the focus has moved from trying to discover any good idea, to trying to deal with a multitude of them.

People need to record all their good ideas and not lose one of them, there is no knowing where breakthroughs will come from. In the end it is important to move through to agreements for implementation.

The degree of powerfulness and creativity in this room is a measure of the clarity of shared ideals and the resolve to abide by them. These are often the most durable products that have come out of the Confusion Room.

Confusion and Renewal are linked. The deeper the first, the stronger the second.

THE CHOICE 5 - SAFE PAST OR RISKY FUTURE

ACKNOWLEDGEMENT TO CLAES JANSSEN AND MARVIN WEISBORD

# Four levels of group maturity

**Level 1 Dependence**

Dependence is very primitive stuff. Most children get out of it by the age of 13. In fact they'll turn their parents from the people they love most into the people they hate the most if they can't move out of dependence. They can no more resist their loathing for dependence than they can resist growing up.

Dependent relationships are un-negotiated. Mature people detest them. The only behaviours they can bring to these relationships are precisely the behaviours they ceased to use at the age of 13. Mummy/Daddy/Boss knows best. To remain in a dependent relationship is a sure path to the tragedy of institutionalisation.

If a bureaucracy is a place where 'no one may do anything unless a person one position higher says they may,' it is a place designed to create dependencies.

Bureaucracy holds people at low levels of group maturity.

ACKNOWLEDGEMENT TO BION

## Level 2 Fight/Flight

Fight /Flight is a higher level of group maturity than dependence because people are not' 'just copping it' any more. There is resistance, either to 'get out' or to 'get at them'. People are looking after themselves better.

Fight: (anger, frustration, hostility). In bad work places some people may go to work just so that they can fight the system. When people feel ripped off, they rip off. Anything from petty theft through to sabotage.

Flight: (fear, anxiety, unassertiveness, apathy and withdrawal). People get sick, become clever at being absent, give up, become slack and retire on the job.

These behaviours are about coping, self preservation and survival. People can be creative in how they do this. The traditional workplace promotes Fight/Flight behaviours when it rewards the 'street-wise', the people with good bureaucratic and political 'footwork'.

That is how old system can easily promote ego rather than talent. In Dependence and Fight/Flight people are concentrating on survival rather than productivity.

ACKNOWLEDGEMENT TO BION

## Level 3 Pairing

Pairing is the first level of group maturity at which people focus on productivity.

In the picture, each crew is in 'Pairing. They are enjoying their freedom and being in a team, they are working hard together and 'doing their best'.

This is the first level of productive behaviour. People have now begun to co-operate and feel motivated. Compared with Dependence and Fight/Flight, Pairing is like healing to the soul.

However, people seldom think past their boundary. At this stage, people may not need to be 'driven', but they may need to be 'steered', at least until they have learned to think and to co-operate across their boundary.

This takes them to Interdependence, the highest level of group maturity.

ACKNOWLEDGEMENT TO BION

## Level 4 Interdependence

Interdependence is the ideal that can become the norm. Here people are in a regular process of negotiating the dependencies which are best for them, their work teams and their work place.

Dependence and Fight/Flight are a natural reaction to autocratic leaders. Pairing and Interdependence require democratic leadership to exist.

The alternatives to autocracy (do as you're told) are either laissez-faire (do as you like) or democracy (we do as we have agreed).

Autocratic and Laissez-Faire behaviours come naturally.

Democratic behaviours have to be learned.

**THE CHOICE 5 - SAFE PAST OR RISKY FUTURE**

ACKNOWLEDGEMENT TO BION

## THE CHOICE 6 - RULES OR RESULTS

- EQUIFINALITY
- MINIMUM CRITICAL SPECIFICATIONS

# Equifinality

Equifinality means there is 'more than one way to get there'. It is essential for the exploration of new 'good ways to do things'. It is the opposite to uniformity and conformity. It acknowledges difference. It supports a search for continuous improvement and creativity.

Equifinality can only occur where managers allow *Everybody* to control their work. Where they have integrated managing and doing. Equifinality occurs where there is humility, and recognition that a breakthrough may occur from the most unexpected quarter.

Equifinality is unnatural to anyone who has been brought up within the old system. It will confront a lot of us for a long time.

In the traditional autocratic workplace managers try to be in control. One way they attempt to administer control is through creating detailed specifications.

The new workplace is built on the belief that control occurs best if it is done by *Everybody* .....within limits.

THE CHOICE 6 - RULES OR RESULTS

## Minimum critical specifications

The old system is designed to create consistency and control. It puts great store by conformity. It achieves this by detailing all possible specifications. This produces consistency and control at the expense of ownership, innovation and the capacity to improve.

The alternative is to specify only the minimum and most critical.
To create Minimum Critical Specifications.

Minimum Critical Specifications can form the boundary within which teams self manage. They make possible the integration of managing and doing. This allows ownership and the capacity to innovate and improve. They make *Everybody* responsible for their relationships, outcomes and customers.

Complexity cannot be managed by striving for simplicity through centralisation and other forms of conformity.

When managing and doing are integrated *Everybody* handles complexity.
Minimum critical Specifications create the boundaries and Equifinality sanctions the space.

# THE CHOICE 7 - THE ENVIRONMENT : DEMOTIVATING OR MOTIVATING

- THE MOTIVATORS
- GIVING DIRECTIONS OR SETTING DIRECTIONS
- ORGANISATIONAL SLUMS
- BEHAVIOUR AND ENVIRONMENT
- THE NEW WORKPLACE RELATIONSHIPS
- INSTITUTIONALISATION

## The motivators

Motivation is the consequence of the interaction between individuals and their environment.

It appears there are six factors which affect our motivation. Autonomy, Variety, Learning, Mutual Support and Respect, Wholeness and Meaning and a Desirable Future.

We can have too much, too little or just the right amount of each of the first three factors, Autonomy (elbow room), Variety and Learning.

These three factors have to do with the individual's relationship to the work itself.

*Everybody* is unique in the amount that is just right for them and this amount changes over time.

ACKNOWLEDGEMENT TO FRED EMERY AND ERIC TRIST

# The motivators

We all want as much as we can get of these three factors. Mutual Support and Respect, Wholeness and Meaning and a Desirable Future relate to the social environment at work and our perspective on the system.

Mutual Support and Respect can be received and can be given.

Meaning comes from knowing how our effort contributes to the whole. It can also be pride that what we do supports what we value.

A Desirable Future follows when what we are doing is getting us to somewhere we want to go, not a dead end job.

*Everybody* knows the range of tasks and settings they find intrinsically motivating.

We may not live to see workplaces in which *Everybody* can be equal humans. But, by designing in the Motivators, we can immediately create work in which *Everybody* can be equally human.

We can do this today.


THE CHOICE 7 - ENVIRONMENT : DEMOTIVATING OR MOTIVATING

ACKNOWLEDGEMENT TO FRED EMERY AND ERIC TRIST

# Giving directions or setting directions

The picture says much about the traditional workplace. The dependent, bored and demeaned crew. The distrusting, exasperated and anxious boss. Although both are necessary to each other, neither gains from each other and they are all directionless and in peril.

Yet the boss is flat out giving directions.

It is only possible to move from giving to setting directions when *Everybody* has the information, autonomy and skills to self manage. The tasks of coordination and control are then transferred to where the work is done.

The substructure of the new work organisation is a self managing work team with 'whole system' or wide task boundaries and information, and with direct links to their customers.

**THE CHOICE 7 - ENVIRONMENT : DEMOTIVATING OR MOTIVATING**

# Organisational slums

Shame is a toxic feeling. It is the product of a sense of defeat, indignity and alienation. It deals with deep psychological distress by giving up. Shame therefore is neither healthy nor self caring. There is no immunity to it. Shame is a lonely inner torment in which the self feels itself as one having a 'sickness of the soul'. It is a health hazard.

The traditional workplace creates power through status. Status is often a measure of relative contempt. The traditional workplace therefore creates an ideal environment for generating shame.

The phrase "I'm only a" can be a sign of shame. "I'm only an operator", "I'm only a junior" or even "I'm only a scientist" or "I'm only a manager". These people are saying they feel inferior. Workplace slums are those places where people feel stuck in a position of inferiority and shame. The people may lack pride in what they do, power to improve what they do or even an understanding of what they do. This is often but not necessarily 'at the bottom'. Most traditional workplaces have slums and people usually feel imprisoned there.

The irony is that slums can be at the core of the productive or value-adding part of the business. The people who are the most dependent are often those upon whom the business is most dependent. In these cases the slum dwellers have only one form of power. To stop work.

THE CHOICE 7 - ENVIRONMENT : DEMOTIVATING OR MOTIVATING

# Behaviour and environment

People's behaviour is shaped by their environment and their need to look after themselves.

The traditional workplace sets out to control people. The focus is on people not their environment. When people are being unproductive, traditional thinking ignores that they are behaving in the best way they can to care for themselves in that environment. It creates rules rather than choices.

The mindset is autocratic control.

The new workplace considers the whole system. It looks at the relationship between the people and their environment. When people are unproductive the new workplace asks the question. "Why do people believe the best way they can look after themselves is to behave in an unproductive manner?"

The mindset is information.

The assumptions of the traditional workplace are that people cannot be trusted and must be driven.

The new workplace knows people's behaviour is linked to their environment. It changes the focus from the people to their environment. It swaps blaming for enquiry.

THE CHOICE 7 - ENVIRONMENT : DEMOTIVATING OR MOTIVATING

# The new workplace relationships   (Sociotechnical systems)

The old system is about *Everybody* being controlled. The new system is about *Everybody* being in control. It is designed to create a whole relationship between people and their technology, a socio-technical system.

This requires information systems that connect *Everybody* to everything they need to know and influence – 'the good oil'. *Everybody* having access to skills so that they can be competent in many ways. *Everybody* linked closely to their customer and the business results.

When *Everybody* can see the whole, they can respond to the whole. They can be responsible.

When the information system connects *Everybody* to the whole their contributions can be counted. They can be accountable.

In the new workplace people control their technology rather than the other way around.


THE CHOICE 7 - ENVIRONMENT : DEMOTIVATING OR MOTIVATING

# Institutionalisation

Sometimes the process of change needs time. Particularly when people have become conditioned by their experience of work. They can become institutionalised and give up thinking, contributing and using initiative. Worse still, they can become traumatised and find it very difficult to have any trust in change. This level of damage usually follows organisations and/or unions becoming thuggish.

THE CHOICE 7 - ENVIRONMENT : DEMOTIVATING OR MOTIVATING

Teams self manage when, within agreed boundaries, they plan, do and review their work, and manage their own discipline. The traditional role of the supervisor then disappears and these people make their contributions in entirely different ways.

Traditional unionism has been a response to bosses that give directions. The new system creates a possibility for unions to contribute to the setting of directions.

# THE CHOICE 8 - LOOKS NEW OR REALLY NEW

- THE OLD SYSTEM IS ALWAYS SEDUCTIVE
- THE FUNDAMENTALS OF WORK DESIGN

## The old system is always seductive

People become frustrated when they know there is something better and they are unable to do anything about it.

The old system has brain-washed us. It has a remarkable ability to reappear in our heads.

That is why we label what's new by what's missing.

For thirty years the radio was called a wireless. For twenty years numerous groups have been practising leadership from within the group. They are still referred to as 'leaderless'. We have had electronic funds transfer for ten years, but it is still 'the cashless economy'.

When will we stop walking around with 'cordless telephones'?

Perhaps at the end of the 'post industrial era'?

THE CHOICE 8 - LOOKS NEW OR REALLY NEW

# The fundamentals of work design

1. Make a shift beyond problem solving to whole system thinking.
2. Focus on the future. Envision the way the organisation could be, rather than the way it has been.
3. Create a workplace capable of continuous learning, improvement and adaptation to change.
4. Design in flexibility by redundancy of skills, rather than of people.
5. Design the whole system, not individual jobs.
6. Design work so *Everybody* is connected to the client.
7. Replace dependency, wherever it occurs, with interdependency.
8. Move away from control by position and status to leadership based on clarity of a shared vision, collaboration, and information exchange.
9. Agree to Minimum Critical Specifications which maximise freedom for people to improve the way they work and adapt to their environment.
10. Structure participation in, not to help people feel good, but to optimise every person's contribution.

THE CHOICE 8 - LOOKS NEW OR REALLY NEW

11. Form work teams which take part in establishing their goals, have the right to determine their unique way to achieve these goals, and the responsibility to co-ordinate with other parts of the organisation.
12. Ensure *Everybody* understands enough about the whole process to be able to influence how it works.
13. Ensure *Everybody* has the autonomy to be able to make improvements without asking for permission.
14. Have *Everybody* help design their work. This includes planning and reviewing the work, as well as doing it.
15. Ensure *Everybody* has satisfactory remuneration and working conditions.
16. Within the context of their team, have *Everybody* design their work so that they can experience the 6 factors which make it intrinsically motivating. These are :
Autonomy, Variety, Learning and Feedback, Mutual Support and Respect, Wholeness and Meaning, and a Desirable Future.

Tony Richardson was born in Britain within the sound of his Dad's mill hooter. He thought it was a nice sound but after working in that industry around the world the hooter became less appealing. He became a clergyman, set up a craft/farming community, worked as a public servant and then became a Visiting Fellow at The Australian National University. It was here that he discovered he'd turned into a consultant. He consults to organisations that involve *Everybody* as they improve their whole system. (Unless they make mill hooters.) He lives in Tasmania, works all over the place, loves to catch fish and paint pictures.

Jock Macneish was born in Trinidad and went to school in Scotland. He studied Architecture in London and in Melbourne and has worked in many parts of the world, including two years in Papua New Guinea. His work covers Architecture, Acoustic Consultancy, Illustrations and Cartooning. He now runs a company that creates images designed to carry ideas. He calls them 'Strategic Images'. He lives in the hills near Melbourne where, if he heard a mill hooter, he'd assume there was a bushfire. He can do without fishing but loves to draw cartoons.

Tony and Jock have collaborated in their work for five years.

# Acknowledgements

Both of us have been helped and supported for years as we have struggled to make work happen in a new way. The ideas of Fred Emery and Marvin Weisbord appear on most pages. Fred Emery is an Australian social scientist who has made a great impact internationally on the design of work. Marvin Weisbord has built on Fred's work and that of his predecessors. Marvin's writings have also made their work accessible to a wider audience.

We are especially grateful to many friends along the way. These include: Margot Gorski, Neil Watson, Colin Pidd, Robert Hockley, Margaret Richardson-Horn, Nigel Tanner, Michael Webb, Martin Taylor, Diana Elton and Nick Parsons.

This guide has evolved over some years. We hope it will continue to evolve. For this to happen it would be helpful to know how it is useful and how it could be improved.

For further reading we suggest an ideal start would be:
Weisbord, M.R. Productive Workplaces: Organizing and Managing for Dignity, Meaning and Community. San Francisco: Jossey-Bass, 1987.

**DON'T PRESS PUBLISHING
AUSTRALIA**